Conflict and

Charles Raven
Team Vicar, St John the Baptist
West Kidderminster Team Ministry

GROVE BOOKS LIMITED
RIDLEY HALL RD CAMBRIDGE CB3 9HU

Contents

1. Introduction 3
2. The Springs of Conflict 5
3. The Church Before Mount Zion 9
4. Facing Conflict 13
5. Conflict and Convergence 17
6. 'On Earth as in Heaven' 24

Acknowledgements

I would like to thank Canon Ian Bunting for his encouragement to write this booklet and the Grove Spirituality Group who have been a great stimulus. The booklet is dedicated to my wife, Gillian, my partner in 'joy and woe.'

The Cover Illustration is by the author

Copyright © Charles Raven 1998

First Impression February 1998
ISSN 0262-799X
ISBN 1 85174 365 0

1
Introduction

My Experience

The life of many parishes seems to be placid enough and generally good-humoured but under the surface there can be fierce conflict, especially around issues of control, leaving many people hurt and bewildered when the suppressed tensions suddenly break out on the surface. As an ordinand my eyes were opened to the hidden strains this imposes when attending a conference for clergy and leaders. After a time of worship and teaching, the speaker began to pray for the clergy. To my amazement many began to weep and sob as the Holy Spirit released them from deep hurts and weariness—conflict had taken its toll. I have never forgotten that experience and after nearly ten years in parochial ministry, including a curacy in industrial West Yorkshire before my present appointment, I know for myself that 'joy and woe are woven fine.' I delight in the way in which I have seen God bringing a growing sense of new life, hope and purpose to his church, but I also bear the scars of the conflict which so often accompanies such changes. New life does not come without cost and I hope this book will encourage others who are wrestling with difficult situations to keep going. I am deeply persuaded that there is a biblical spirituality robust enough to set leaders and congregations free from weariness and fear for spiritual maturity and effective mission.

Of course, some of the difficulties we experience are the ordinary tensions, personality clashes, factions, jealousies and plain misunderstanding that afflict any human grouping. I am not trying to explain or analyse every type of conflict in the church. But I have come to learn, sometimes painfully, that much more attention needs to be given to the spiritual dimension of these conflicts, because the church is a quite unique form of community.

The Uniqueness of the Church

Spirituality is essential to understanding conflict in the church simply because the church is first and foremost a spiritual community. Paul writes of Christians as those who 'are being built together to become a dwelling where God dwells by his Spirit' (Eph 2.22). Our starting point must be with God himself, seeing the church not as a human initiative but unique among all human institutions as brought into being and sustained by the presence of God himself. The attention given to Paul's metaphor of the church as the body of Christ has tended to obscure the radical implications for today's church of the temple imagery—of both Jesus and Paul—with its rich Old Testament connotations of God's indwelling presence with his people. In Christ, God has 'tabernacled' among his people in a completely new way (John 1.14), in a body, a truth which John makes completely explicit (John 2.19-21), but is also strongly implicit in the synoptics (see, for example, Mark 14.57, 15.29 and parallels in Matt 26.61, 27.39).

The temple has been redefined—by Jesus himself—as his body. This means that Paul's metaphor of the body can never be reduced simply to a call to human beings to work in harmony. What makes the body of Christ distinctive is the presence of God by his Spirit. So Paul, taking the Corinthians to task for their personality cults, reminds them sternly 'Don't you know that you yourselves are God's temple and that God's Spirit lives in you? If anyone destroys God's temple, God will destroy him; for God's temple is sacred and you are that temple' (1 Cor 3.16, 17). The church is to be a living spiritual organism, indwelt by the Holy Spirit, which makes the presence of God manifest, but like the human body it can become diseased.

A Modern Analogy of Health and Sickness

In the body there is conflict between antibodies and the organisms which bring disease. When the immune system malfunctions, sickness and possibly death follows. This breakdown can happen in two ways. The immune system may simply fail, and AIDS shows only too clearly the tragic results as the body eventually succumbs to infections that would never normally be life threatening. Similarly, the absence of conflict in the church does not necessarily indicate health—it may be that it has simply lost the will and/or the discernment to resist the infiltration of spiritual death. Alternatively, antibodies may start to destroy healthy tissue, as in the case of rheumatic fever, and similarly there can be the tragedy of conflict in which committed Christians may end up destroying each other.

This book is an attempt to explore what the church's immune system might look like and presents us with three basic questions:

a) How do we exercise spiritual discernment to distinguish between conflict that is simply destructive and that which is part of a process of restoring the spiritual vitality of the local church?
b) How do we respond creatively and grow through conflict?
c) What does the experience of conflict mean for the reshaping of Anglican identity? In particular, can the issues of spirituality thrown up by conflict give pointers towards a way of being the church which enables convergence rather than fragmentation?

2
The Springs of Conflict

One of the most revealing experiences of conflict I have experienced was a day away for a Church Council. The aim was an exploration of a new phase in the church's life. What actually happened was an explosion of anger and resentment. It was summed up in an exchange between two members of the congregation, one claiming that there had been—unspecified—radical changes, the other that there had been no changes. In fact both were right—the outward arrangements of the church had hardly changed, but the spiritual climate was changing profoundly. Afterwards the church did grow in terms of giving, new members and, for some, in spiritual maturity, but an undercurrent of fierce hostility persisted and even those who felt most antagonism were still not able to articulate their reasons in a way which went even part way to explain their feelings.

When we encounter conflict in the church which seems to be unreasonable or irrational, one obvious response is simply to attribute it to demonic attack. But, while being aware of the reality of spiritual warfare, it is important not to 'demonize' those who oppose us. The demonic does not operate in a vacuum, but finds opportunity in sinful attitudes and patterns of behaviour which can affect all the participants.

Discerning the Real and the Counterfeit

A deeper appreciation of the spiritual dynamics of conflict is given in a fascinating series of contrasts drawn by Paul in Galatians 4.21ff. To a church which is in mortal danger of apostasy and religious legalism, Paul pleads passionately for a recovery of their true freedom in Christ. The allegory of the two women, Hagar and Sarah, is a powerful statement of the difference between human religiosity—a counterfeit gospel (Gal 1.7)—and living faith. Here are two quite distinct ways of being the church and without constant spiritual vigilance, any church—however radical its origins—tends towards 'Ishmael' rather than 'Isaac.' Paul piles up Old Testament motifs with such rapidity that we are left somewhat breathless and in danger of missing the richness of this sustained contrast. So, for the sake of clarity, the allegory is set out as follows:

	Counterfeit Church	**True Church**
The sons…	Ishmael	Isaac
…who are the result of…	Unbelief	Promise
The mothers…	Hagar	Sarah
…who represent	The Old Covenant[1]	The New Covenant
The spiritual homes of the false and true church	Old Jerusalem (this worldly)	New Jerusalem (heaven—the kingdom of God)
status	Slaves	Children of God
lifestyle	slavery	freedom
creative principle	human nature	the power of the Spirit

The power of this allegory is in the way it draws out the radical consequences of being justified by faith—not only is the Christian given a new standing with God, but enters into a wholly different way of life characterized by freedom, trust and the power of the Spirit. And Paul is clear that wherever these two modes of being the church co-exist, there will inevitably be conflict (v 29). The church which lives in the power of the Spirit will reveal, just by its existence, the emptiness and spiritual bankruptcy of religion which becomes a striving after human ideals. It disturbs relationships and power structures which have been built on this false foundation, calling forth a deep hostility to that which is seen as threatening. Genuine spiritual growth and conflict are therefore inseparable and any real movement of the Holy Spirit will at some point be a 'sign spoken against' (Lk 2.34). Indeed, the absence of such conflict could lead us to question whether there was in fact any spiritual life at all. It is in this sense I believe we should understand Karl Barth's comment that 'A real church cannot possibly fail to see that it is only a theatre of conflict between the true church and the false.'[2] But what is the nature of this conflict in the church?

---

1   This does not mean that the Mt Sinai Covenant was in any way false, simply that it has now been superseded.
2   K Barth, *Church Dogmatics Volume 4, Part 1* (Edinburgh: T&T Clark, 1956) p 708.

Whose Church?

This is the radical question posed by Paul's allegory. Are we going to take matters into our own hands, trusting in our own effort and moral insight, or are we going to exercise faith, trusting in God's promises and living by the power of the Spirit? A watershed in my previously sceptical attitude towards the charismatic renewal was an address by John Wimber on the theme 'God wants his church back.' This is a principle which touches every aspect of the Christian life, from the individual's prayer life to the development of theology and the structures of the church. It is also a vital principle in dealing with conflict.

In our battles we can be rather like Joshua before the battle of Jericho. When the Lord appears to him as a man with a drawn sword, Joshua asks 'Are you for us or our enemies?' but the reply is 'Neither, but as commander of the army of the Lord I have now come' (Joshua 5.13,14). Joshua's immediate reaction is to determine whether or not this formidable figure is on his side, but the Lord has not come to take sides—he has come to take charge. And the one who quite understandably thought that he was the commander of the Lord's army falls to the ground in reverence. It is essential to be clear on this point before moving on to bring into sharper focus the spiritual contours of conflict. While we will inevitably come into conflict with other people we must avoid fighting personal battles.

Bonhoeffer's Razor

This is not a reference to a holy relic! It is a principle of spiritual discernment found in the first chapter of Dietrich Bonhoeffers' book *Life Together*,[3] a profoundly scriptural reflection on his own experience of Christian community as the head of a seminary of the German 'Confessing Church' at Finkenwalde (now part of Poland). His ministry there inspired many of the pastors who resisted Hitler.[4] It was written in the late 1930s well before the modern charismatic movement had begun to impinge on the theological consciousness of mainstream denominations and challenges equally what passes for 'normal' Christianity and its charismatic or pentecostal expressions.

Although in a very different context, he is confronting with penetrating insight the same basic issue as Wimber—the fundamental reality that the church is something called into being by God which we have no right to take into our own hands. For Bonhoeffer, authentic Christian life together 'depends upon its being clear right from the beginning, *first, that Christian brotherhood is not an ideal, but a divine reality. Second, that Christian brotherhood is a spiritual and not a psychic reality.*'[5]

---

3 Dietrich Bonhoeffer, *Life Together* (London: SCM Press, 1954).
4 For the background to this see Lawrence Osborn, *Discernment* (Grove Spirituality booklet 63) page 21ff.
5 *op cit*, p 15 (italics as original).

The first principle of discernment, *'that Christian brotherhood is not an ideal, but a divine reality'* recognizes that Christian community is not something we can create; it can only be received through response to God's Word. For Bonhoeffer, its point was to protect the community from the false visionary who tries to control it in order to achieve his own ideals. This becomes a denial of God's grace, a subtle form of taking into our own hands that which belongs to God. In this case, failure of the vision is the best thing which can happen because it reminds everyone that the real scriptural foundation of all Christian community is God's forgiveness and our adoption by grace. The community is not held together by shared religious feelings or by achieving a certain level of piety, but simply by faith in God's grace, accepting one another on the same basis as we know God to have accepted us.

The second principle of discernment *'that Christian brotherhood is a spiritual and not a psychic reality'* expresses the crucial role of the Holy Spirit. The Christian community is unique. 'Because Christian community is founded solely on Jesus Christ, it is a spiritual and not a psychic reality. In this it differs absolutely from all other communities. The Scriptures call "pneumatic," "spiritual," that which is created only by the Holy Spirit, who puts Jesus Christ into our hearts as Lord and Saviour. The Scriptures term "psychic," "human," that which comes from the natural urges, powers, and capacities of the human spirit.'[6] This is a contrast of some subtlety and it will be expanded below. Here we simply need to note that it is not Bonhoeffer's intention to suggest that the normal human affections that exist in marriage, family or friendship are to be rejected, but that they do not provide a proper model for the church since they are so much bound up with human needs and desires. For instance, it seems to me that talk of the 'church family' tends to encourage an exclusive attitude within a congregation and inhibits a genuine interest in evangelism which might disrupt 'the family' by new additions. The Holy Spirit creates the Christian community by bringing into our experience the new identity which we have as children of God. It is his work to free us from all false dependencies, including the need to manipulate and control the love of others to establish our sense of worth. We are free to serve one another in a way which is not undermined by manipulation and the creation of dependent relationships.

Bonhoeffer's 'razor' is therefore the crucial ability to discern the difference between authentic Christian life and that which is the projection of human ideals and aspirations. The razor has two blades—it is based on a biblical spirituality of both Word and Spirit and without it the church is heading for spiritual death. 'The existence of any Christian life together depends on whether it succeeds at the right time in bringing out the ability to distinguish between a human ideal and God's reality, between spiritual and human community.'[7]

[6] *Life Together*, p 19.
[7] *op cit*, p 24.

3
The Church Before Mount Zion

The church lives between the 'already' of new life won by Christ and the 'not yet' of its complete visible fulfilment. This eschatological perspective is crucial to maintaining a sense of balance, not simply accepting the church as it is, but neither becoming terminally discouraged by its imperfections. The writer to the Hebrews reminds the church of her destiny and purpose. 'But you have come to Mount Zion, to the heavenly Jerusalem, the city of the living God' (Heb 12.22). We have already come across the metaphor of the city, the contrast between the heavenly Jerusalem, the Christian's spiritual home, and the old Jerusalem—the church which lives by faith, looks to the heavenly Jerusalem as its mother (Gal 4.26), the city where its members truly belong. The City of God is the place of God's presence and rule recognized by faith because it is a divine reality, the church as the joyful assembly of men and angels before Mount Zion, the heavenly Jerusalem. It is as the church comes before Mount Zion in reverence and adoration that it becomes most truly itself. And to come before Mount Zion means:

a) *We know that we have not yet arrived.* The City of God is an eschatological reality which is still unfolding and cannot be identified exclusively with any particular church or institution. Yet it is the Christian's true home and we are called to live now as ambassadors for Christ, not simply in evangelism, but in a whole way of life. This means that there will always be an element of ambiguity in the church as its members continue to feel the pull of this-worldly values even though they have a foretaste of the new order. Augustine's distinction between the the City of God and the earthly city is very helpful at this point because he provides us with a way of looking at the church which is inclusive but not complacent about the extent to which the church can be subverted. His great work *The City of God* was a sustained response to pagan critics who attributed the sack of Rome in 410 to the abandonment of the old pagan religions. The traditional allegory of the two cities—Jerusalem and her ancient enemy Babylon—is developed to set Jerusalem, the 'City of God,' animated by a radical love of God, in contrast with Babylon, the 'earthly city' animated by a radical love of self. The two cities also represent the spiritual allegiance of individuals, either to Christ or the devil. But since the devil is able to disguise himself as an angel of light (2 Cor 11.15), so are the citizens of his city. So Augustine is clear that any attempt to set up a true church on the basis of the holiness of its members is highly dangerous: 'The manifest separation of these two peoples and two cities will be when the harvest is winnowed; until which times love bears with every part of the crop, lest while those who are the grain too hastily flee from the chaff, they impiously separate themselves from others of the grain.'[8] For Augustine, this was a vital step in preserving the unity of the catholic church. In our own day, we need to regain this perspective that *'love bears with every part of the crop'* if the fragmented body of Christ is to recover its unity, while not losing sight of the urgent need for the church to reflect the values and priorities of the City of God.

b) *We are acknowledging that the church should live by divine rather than human initiative.* The fulfilment of the promise to Abraham is the 'city with foundations, whose architect and builder is God' (Heb 11.10). Seen in this perspective the church needs to be constantly guided by the 'architecture' of the biblical revelation cenç ed on CÅ;ist. It also needs to be built by God, manifested as a divine and not simply human initiative through the endless creativity of the Holy Spirit. Although God's ultimate purpose will not be thwarted, there is nothing automatic about this process. There is no guarantee that any particular church will be faithful to the gospel or consistently live by the power of the Spirit rather than the spirit of the age. Realistic discernment recognizes that 'Ishmael' may supplant 'Isaac,' that 'Babylon' may infiltrate 'Jerusalem,' in both the dimensions of Word and Spirit, subverting the work of the one who is both architect and builder. The matrix below illustrates what can happen.

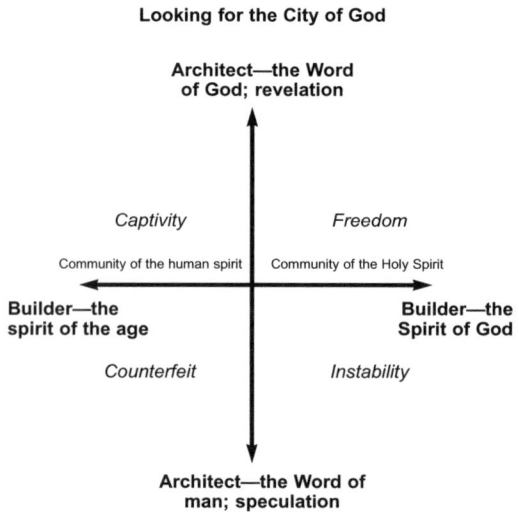

---

8 Cited in Gerald Bonner, *St Augustine of Hippo, Life and Controversies* (Norwich: Canterbury Press, 1963) p 289.

The church as the community of the Holy Spirit, built on the Word of God and built by the Spirit of God is represented by the upper right quadrant. Its hallmark is freedom because the community of the Spirit exists by God's grace, not human achievement or merit, and people can relate to each other freely as children of God. Its counterfeit is the lower left quadrant where delight in exploring God's revelation has been replaced by clever speculation and the church has become captive to the spirit of the age. Perhaps the Church of England has a particular vulnerability to both these tendencies. Church life of this type may appear to be quite successful, humanly speaking. It may not necessarily sponsor glaring heresies and may have strong ethical commitments, but it will be unable to draw people to Christ and will be preoccupied with its own needs and survival. The two quadrants are fundamentally different modes of being the church and Paul recognizes the reality that there is a an inevitable abrasion between them, between that which flows from the divine initiative in the power of the Holy Spirit and that which is man's initiative (Gal 4.29). The work of God will always challenge human pride and the systems that flow from human speculation.

But before looking at the manifestations of this conflict in detail, it is worth remembering that the decay of the community of the Spirit can occur in more subtle ways than the sharp contrast between the upper right and lower left quadrants. The upper left quadrant represents the 'Ephesian' tendency (Revelation 2.1-7), the temptation of the conservative church where there is a zeal for sound doctrine and morality, but where these values degenerate into an unattractive and controlling legalism to be promoted by methods which encourage faction and party spirit. On the other hand, the lower right quadrant represents the 'Sardis' tendency (Revelation 3.1-6), the vulnerability of the charismatic church to an unstable and potentially lethal accommodation with the surrounding culture when it loses its grip on God's Word and lives off a reputation for success and innovation. This is hardly a common problem in Anglican parishes, but the fate of the Sheffield 'Nine O'clock Service' may be a warning for the future.

The particular manifestations of conflict between the 'Ishmael' and 'Isaac' tendencies in church life will take many forms. But Bonhoeffer approaches the heart of the matter when he writes, 'Human love cannot tolerate the dissolution of a fellowship that has become false for the sake of genuine fellowship' because it is based simply on the natural desire for community and 'so long as it can satisfy this desire in some way, it will not give up, even for the sake of truth, even for the sake of the genuine love for others. But where it can no longer expect its desire to be fulfilled, there it stops short—namely in the face of an enemy. There it turns into hatred, calumny and contempt.'[9] This comment sheds a vast amount of light on the sometimes perplexing and contradictory behaviour

---

9 *Life Together*, p 22.

which occurs when spiritual growth is taking place and substitute religiosity is revealed for what it truly is. When aspects of a church's life which have been built without a dependence upon Word and Spirit are challenged, we can expect two characteristic responses:

a) *A Disregard for Truth*

The need to preserve the religious 'club' and the status of its inner circle becomes paramount. This was brought home to me in a rather startling way when a puzzled churchwarden once said to me 'People (sic) are saying "Why do we keep getting these sermons about Jesus?"' There may be a superficial concern for unity, but it will be an inclusiveness without real content which is energized by what it is against. This is a particular problem where congregations have lost their grounding in Scripture and tradition and been encouraged to adopt a 'pick-and-mix' approach to their faith, believing what feels right without much real interest as to whether or not it is actually true.

b) *The Persistence of Conflict*

Where the fellowship of a church has been based on the fulfilment of needs under the guise of religion rather than a common commitment to Jesus Christ and experience of the Holy Spirit, sooner or later there comes a point when it dawns on people that a choice must be made. Those who opt to cling to the counterfeit tend to retreat further and further into unreality and will continue to resist change even when it involves contradictory and apparently irrational behaviour. Alternating from friendship to hostility, or holding on to positions of influence while declining to contribute financially, will be guided by one aim, to try and retain as much control over the church as possible. This need to retain control may even turn into hysterical behaviour if it is unsuccessful. Paradoxically, people who appeared to be part of a loving fellowship can become seriously hostile, but this is at root simply because they are losing something they should never have possessed in the first place, a fellowship of the self-centred which, for all its inclusive language, is actually very exclusive to those who do not abide by its rules.

4
Facing Conflict

The value—and challenge—of Paul's powerful allegory in Galatians and Bonhoeffer's insight into the uniqueness of Christian community is the realization that the integrity of the church cannot be guaranteed by static formularies of church order and denominational confessions, necessary though they may be. Our life together has a dynamic and personal dimension as something which God brings into being and constitutes by the Holy Spirit. The struggle between 'Ishmael' and 'Isaac' is played out within each individual Christian as well as the church as we participate in a process of spiritual growth. No one individual or church will ever be completely 'authentic'—but they can move in that direction. For those in positions of leadership, this is to enter a spiritual 'multi-gym' which at times will take us to the limits of what we feel we can endure, but through perseverance and God's grace we can be more than survivors as God reshapes our attitudes.

The Dispositions of the City of God: In Conflict
1. Freedom

Isaac is the son of the free woman and freedom is a key theme of the New Testament, especially for Paul. The freedom which Christians enjoy is freedom from condemnation, legalism and the fear of death and freedom to (paradoxically) submit their lives to Christ. This freedom is based on the promise of the Word of God and comes into our experience through the Spirit of God. 'Where the Spirit of the Lord is, there is freedom. And we with unveiled faces, beholding the glory of the Lord, are being transformed from one degree of glory to another' (2 Cor 3.17–18). Sooner or later such freedom will 'smoke out' the informal power structures which flow from the human instinct to control and manipulate others. Much as Pharaoh sought to keep the Hebrews in slavery for his own ends, refusing Moses' request to worship, this sort of controlling spirit will refuse to allow others to have freedom, especially in worship, because diversity in the church threatens their control. My policy has been to encourage diversity in worship, recognizing the need for 'safe places' both for those who need to explore worship and Scripture in an atmosphere of faith and openness and also for those who feel threatened if familiar liturgical landmarks are removed.

Those with a strong experience and theology of the Holy Spirit are not immune from such controlling attitudes. Bonhoeffer warns that in the human community of spirit, as opposed to the community of the Spirit, it is possible that 'there rules, along with the Word, the man who is furnished with exceptional powers, experience and magical suggestive capacities.'[10] Such people may be devout and well-intentioned, but the result of their attempts to bind other people to themselves is to quench the Holy Spirit and make his presence seem remote. I find something deeply unattractive about churches which claim to be Spirit-led, but are much more the expression of a particular leader's personality. How does leadership which is dedicated to true freedom chart a path through these minefields?

a) *By rejecting all forms of personality cult*—and the patterns of subtle manipulation that go with it. The need to be loved and liked is very strong in most leaders and can lead them into allowing tracts of time to be taken up with trying to keep everyone happy. The Revd Martin Down, commenting on pressures in his churches in rural Norfolk, succinctly observed: 'It is not my job, it is not the job of a Christian leader, to keep everybody happy. My job is to keep God happy. And if people get upset, well I am sorry about it, but there does come a point where you have to say "Well, that's the way it is."'[11] A spirit of control needs to be met with the contrary spirit of service and freedom. Church fellowship can easily be built upon human affinity rather than upon the common affinity of the indwelling Holy Spirit. When this happens, a controlling and unhealthy intimacy enters the life of the church, whether it be in a group who meet in the pub or the prayer meeting. The intimacy that flows from restored relationships will produce the fruit of the Spirit, not manipulation, fear and insecurity.

b) *By resisting the temptation of power-play.* This can be very difficult when dealing with people who are highly controlling and have sophisticated political skills. The temptation to meet 'fire with fire,' can be very powerful, but usually backfires. Leadership of a church through a process of significant change does require certain positive management skills, for instance in terms of communication, sensitivity to changing attitudes and the identification of gifts. What it does not need are the darker political arts of manipulation and control. Such strategies need to be rigorously rejected. They breed distrust and because such powerful spiritual dynamics are unleashed by real change, those who are looking to find fault will pounce on any perceived inconsistency.

c) *By knowing when to speak and when to be silent.* There are times when controlling and abusive behaviour in the church has to be resisted openly by speaking the truth. At times, Jesus himself was sharply controversial in his criticism of the religious elite of his day. There will be times when conflict has to be faced openly for the sake of the health of the body of Christ to allow issues to be brought out into the light. David Watson makes the point with his cus-

10 *Life Together,* p 19.
11 *Vicarage Allsorts*—BBC Radio 4, 2.7.97.

tomary clarity: 'Satan can play on our weaknesses so that we become peace-lovers rather than peace-makers. We avoid conflict; we fail to resolve tensions in relationships; we allow sin to continue within the fellowship without being challenged; we agree with all points of view in a muddy ecumenism instead of clear unity in Christ. Christ the bridegroom looks for moral and doctrinal purity in his bride, the church.'[12]

There is also the time to be silent. When to speak and when to be silent is ultimately something we sense through prayer and the guidance of the Holy Spirit rather than analysis. There have been occasions when I have felt a strong check in my spirit not to speak which has gone entirely against my natural instincts. I have sat silently through meetings where I have known that people were being deliberately misled or where my own reputation was being attacked, trusting in God's ability to protect his church—and me! However justified the intention, controversy that is not of the Holy Spirit leads people into destructive faction and gives a foothold to evil.

2. Meekness
a) *Surrender*

The starting point for true discernment and any real resolution of conflict is the place of surrender. It is no coincidence that Paul prefaces his outworking of the analogy of the body of Christ in Romans 12 by urging the brethren to 'offer your bodies as living sacrifices' which will enable them to 'test and approve what God's will is' (Rom 12.1, 2). This surrender applies to all levels of Christian living. It includes the intellectual humility of acknowledging that the 'foolishness of God is wiser than man's wisdom' (1 Cor 1.25) and much damage is done to the body of Christ by those within the church's leadership who play clever language games with Scripture and tradition to accommodate fundamental Christian doctrines and moral teaching to the spirit of the age. But conflict in the church is not simply a product of theological faultlines. There is also the spiritual surrender of our lives to Christ as Lord of the church. Those with sound doctrine and outstanding spiritual gifts are not immune from using these things as the vehicle of powerful egos. Paul has to rebuke the Corinthian church because their conflicts were of a kind that showed they were acting as 'mere men' who had to be addressed as 'worldly' rather than 'spiritual' (1 Cor 3.1–3) despite their enthusiastic use of abundant spiritual gifts and their pride in their wisdom. Indeed Paul later makes the very radical statement that a church may possess all these things and yet be without any real value, even offensive, if there is no love, that most excellent way of the Spirit (1 Cor 13.1-3). The third Beatitude promises that the meek will inherit the earth (Matt 5.5), and it is this quality of humble dependence on God which I believe is absolutely crucial if we

---

12 David Watson, *Discipleship* (Hodder & Stoughton, 1981) p 176.

are to work though conflict constructively. If we are clinging on to our supposed rights—for instance of reputation, career or security—we are always going to be vulnerable to manipulation, of others and by others.

b) *Authority*

This may seem strange under the heading of 'meekness,' but I include it because the authority of any Christian leader comes from his or her submission to Christ. It is not a right and it does not ultimately depend on the leader's qualities—it is bestowed by God for the upbuilding of the church. This seems to be the point of the various offices listed in the fivefold ministry of Ephesians 4.11-13. And it is interesting to note that Moses, who exercised awesome authority as liberator and lawgiver is described as 'very meek above all the men which were upon the face of the earth' (Numbers 12.3). Leaders can be inhibited by a common misunderstanding of servant leadership. A prominent lay person once said to me, 'You are here to serve us, so that means you must do what we want.' But this ends up with the church being dominated by the strongest personalities. Leadership which is first and foremost submitted to Christ will not be weak. I am indebted to Robert Warren for the insight that whereas Jesus was tough with the strong and gentle with the weak, human nature is to be compliant when dealing with the strong and tough when dealing with the weak. Servanthood is in the first instance being a servant of Jesus Christ, the servant king, exercising the authority that comes from submission to him.

c) *Prayer*

By giving priority to prayer, we give concrete and sacrificial expression to meekness. We recognize that God has a particular way for his work to be done which demonstrates his presence and relies on his power. Conflict emerges when leaders, however well intentioned, seek to carry out God's will in their way and their strength thereby creating an 'Ishmael.' Ishmael was in fact blessed by God (Gen 21.18), but lived in continual conflict with Isaac. If we are not prepared to wait for God to act and take matters into our own hands, we miss God's best and may well sow the seeds for unnecessary conflict. In my own situation it has been very important not to try and impose new worship styles on congregations, but first to allow the truth of the gospel and the the work of the Holy Spirit to percolate through the existing worship patterns. Prayer is also vital in discerning God's will at critical moments. There was a point in my ministry when I was strongly tempted to enter into a legal and media skirmish on behalf of someone I felt to have been seriously wronged, but drew back through the prayerful counsel of people close to me. With hindsight I now see the destructive consequences which might well have flowed from a decision which would have been justified in principle but was not generated in prayer. The willingness to entrust our hopes to God and not take matters into our own hands is often referred to in Scripture as 'waiting'—see Isaiah 30.18, Ps 40.1. This is definitely not the soft option. It can mean you run the gauntlet between those who are impatient to move on and those who resist all change, but it is vital if the spiritual life of the church is to have enduring quality. It seems to be characteristic of God's working—one of the marks of his glory—that he turns situations upside down and does that which is humanly unpredictable and surprising. The quotation from Isaiah 54.1 which erupts into the middle of Paul's sophisticated allegory of Hagar and Sarah in Galatians (4.27) encapsulates wonderfully both the labour of waiting and the exultant joy of new birth, that sense of suffering and victory which seems to be the hallmark of genuine movements of the Holy Spirit.

5
Conflict and Convergence

As the church's 'immune system' begins to function more strongly, 'Ishmael' unwittingly trains 'Isaac'—in the process of renewal and conflict we learn to prize more highly those things which are life-giving and sustaining. By drawing these together we can develop a model of spirituality which may actually enable the church to move towards unity, stability and sustained growth. Along with the inevitable controversy, any genuine work of the Holy Spirit will also bring a new sense of unity and mission. One of the very positive developments of the charismatic renewal within the Church of England and Episcopal churches more widely has been its contribution to a realization that the historically polarized Evangelical and Catholic traditions can complement each other as both are refreshed and enlivened by a new experience of the Holy Spirit. Taking a hint from this development I want to suggest a model of spirituality for the church based on three priorities.

The Priorities of the City of God: In Growth
1. Kerygma
This is a noun derived from a Greek verb used in the New Testament meaning 'to proclaim,' and in normal usage was associated with a particular event, typically a military victory. It encapsulates the basic biblical conviction that lives are transformed through the proclamation of the Word, the message of the gospel. It also reminds us that the gospel is about a salvation which unfolded through the acts of God in history, and not through religious speculation. To live in this

perspective reinforces a major shift in Anglican understanding which is already underway. Historically, the proclamation of the Word has been seen as having a primarily pastoral function in nurturing the faithful because the Church of England, as a national church, came into being at a time when church and society were virtually coterminus. This is now a dangerous illusion and the historic churches are now beginning to face the need to rebuild congregations around the priority of mission and evangelism. Robert Warren comments: 'Building the faith community seems to be central to what the writers of the epistles saw as evangelism…What is easily overlooked is that the church is the primary agent of mission.'[13] If it can shake itself free from its own historical illusions, historic Anglicanism has a key role in presenting Christian faith as public truth in a society which has great difficulty in recognizing moral and religious values as anything more than relative. As we approach the Millennium there is an urgent need for a strong biblical spirituality which can undergird a recovery of that meaning for society as a whole which is enshrined in our marking of time as *'Anno Domini.'* It represents an agreed way of doing theology—tested by the open Bible—but retains the flexibility to present the kerygma in ways that are relevant to the culture.

'Kerygmatic' churches will organize their lives around this sense of mission and immerse themselves in the Scriptures as the 'family history' of God's people, that which gives shape to their lives and a unifying sense of common purpose. For Bonhoeffer, the unity of the Christian community in practice is based on the regular reading together of Scripture. His words have a very contemporary ring: 'We must know the Scriptures first and foremost for the sake of our salvation. But besides this there are ample reasons that make this requirement exceedingly urgent. How, for example, shall we ever attain certainty and confidence in our personal and church activity if we do not stand on solid biblical ground? It is not our heart that determines our course, but God's Word. But who in this day has any understanding of the need for scriptural proof? How often do we hear innumerable arguments "from life" and "from experience" put forward as the basis for the most crucial decisions, but the argument of Scripture is missing.'[14] This centrality of Scripture is reflected in the Anglican emphasis upon the public reading of Scripture (see also Articles 6 and 20) and the practice of saying the daily offices. The commitment to meeting daily to focus on the Scriptures has been a great strength in helping the clergy of my own team ministry to continue working together in sometimes testing circumstances.

---

13 Robert Warren, *Building Missionary Congregations* (CHP, 1995) pp 1,2.
14 Bonhoeffer, *Life Together*, p 39.

2. Charism

This noun comes from the Greek New Testament word for grace and is used to describe the gifts of grace, the gifts of the Holy Spirit. It is through the gift and gifts of the Holy Spirit that the church begins to experience the fact that it is a unique form of community. Although the Holy Spirit is given to individuals, the purpose of the gift of the Holy Spirit is to initiate those individuals into the church and the reality of the kingdom. All four gospels record John the Baptist as the one who describes Jesus as 'baptizing in the Holy Spirit' and Christians are those who are 'born of the Spirit' (John 3.8). So significant was this experience for the first Christians that Paul can appeal to it in his passionate call to the Galatians to turn away from the legalism threatening their community: 'Are you so foolish? After beginning with the Spirit, are you now trying to attain your goal by human effort?' (Gal 3.3). Perhaps much the same could be said to large sections of today's church.

Without the ministry of the Spirit, a church cannot really describe itself as fully Trinitarian, and it is the ministry of the Spirit to call forth diversity within the unity of the body of Christ. If the church is to grow it needs to function in the way God intends. His presence is absolutely crucial because the ministry of the Spirit gives substance to the statement that God is builder of his church. And this ministry brings harmony because the necessary institutional aspects of the church's life are (as it were) 'lubricated' by God's grace. In a church structured around charisms, people will be in positions of leadership because they exercise a ministry not because they seek status or control, or as rewards for hard work. They are recognized as being equipped by the Holy Spirit for a particular function and freed to fulfil it, perhaps even having a taste of Augustine's famous phrase 'whose service is perfect freedom'! The same changes in society which make it imperative for the church to focus upon the 'kerygma' also make it urgent that the church as the 'community of the Spirit' rediscovers the ministry of the Holy Spirit through which the church is equipped for its mission. Anglicanism has shared the spiritual 'blind spot' of Western Christendom to this ministry. Alastair McGrath reflects this widely held assessment when he notes that 'the experiential deficit of classical Anglican thought is well known and was no small contributing cause to the rise of Methodism.'[15] In our own time, the Church of England barely manages to maintain its membership and accounts for a diminishing share in a burgeoning 'market' in spirituality represented by the rise of the New Age movement with its rather irrational and chaotic spirituality. It is even more pressing than ever that Anglicanism has a strong understanding and experience of the Holy Spirit for the sake of its unity and effective mission.

---

15 A McGrath, *The Renewal of Anglicanism* (London: SPCK, 1993) p 78.

3. Sacrament

A sacrament is a sacred sign which is also a vehicle of God's grace. The gospel sacraments of baptism and communion are essential rituals in which the church outwardly expresses its identity and through which God strengthens that identity. The role of sacraments is to continually call the church back to a living relationship with God who is present and to remind the church that the visible expression of its life and unity is important. The sacraments of baptism and communion are instituted by Christ himself as defining actions which give the church in the world its institutional identity. However, from the earliest times there seems to have been a tension between the institutional and charismatic strands of the church's life. Towards the end of the first century a strongly sacramental emphasis arose, often referred to as 'Early Catholicism.' For instance, when we compare Clement's first epistle to the Corinthians written just forty years after Paul's epistles, we find he uses the same metaphor of the body, but it has completely lost Paul's vision of organic interaction. The principle of unity is that of ordered military hierarchy. The eucharist is to be offered with the same care and precision as the temple sacrifices in Jerusalem and the offices of Bishop and Deacon are seen as divine appointments fulfilling Old Testament prophecy![16] But we should not be too quick to see this development as simply a quenching of the Holy Spirit's fire because it is clear from the New Testament itself that this process began through a need to guard the truth of the gospel (eg 1 Tim 3, Titus 1.5-9).

One of the contemporary reasons for this negative attitude towards institutions is the widely held view that Pentecost is the birthday of the church. This is to misunderstand the Old Testament background to the new. There is a continuity which can be traced from Abraham—the church is the 'ekklesia,' the community, which began with the covenant with Abraham and is intended to be a continuing visible physical community in the world. Indeed Paul sees the outpouring of the Holy Spirit as the fulfilment of the promises to Abraham (Gal 3.14). Sacraments, like the charisms, are a visible manifestation of invisible realities and both need to be honoured as such for the health and balance of the church. While the charisms represent the living action of God the Holy Spirit, by nature they can, in isolation, be ambiguous and are capable of being counterfeited. On the other hand, the sacraments are an unambiguous representation of God's presence, but do not guarantee simply by their performance, that the reality of that presence becomes a living experience for those who participate.

Convergence Spirituality

By bringing together these three priorities as complementary, we have a model of spirituality which:

---

[16] See M Staniforth (tr), *1 Clement 37 in Early Christian Writings* (Penguin, 1968) p 42.

a) enables convergence and the resolution of conflict without adopting the bland compromise of the 'lowest common denominator.'
b) enhances the plausibility of the gospel in a culture which is increasingly aware of its spiritual emptiness, but does not look to conventional Christianity.
c) brings together the charismatic and institutional aspects of the church's life on the common basis of grace.

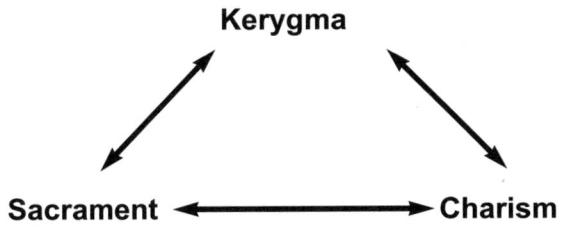

I have quite deliberately not used the terms 'Evangelical,' 'Charismatic' and 'Catholic.' This is partly because I believe the terms I have used refer to that which is actually transformative in the life of the church. They point us to the actions of God's revelation and grace itself, rather than carrying the inevitable party associations of the more familiar words. The second reason is that they are more generic terms, denoting fundamental concepts, which I hope will make the model more flexible. The reality is that different people will have a considerable variety of understandings of the kerygma, of charisms and of sacraments, but what is important is to embark on the convergence process because each element reinforces the other. For instance, there have been attempts to 'demythologize' the kerygma, stripping out those supernatural elements of the early church's proclamation which were thought to belong to an outdated first-century world view. But the experience of charisms in the church sends us back to the New Testament with a sense of excitement that it may actually be able to challenge a materialistic world view.

Leadership and Oversight
The convergence of kerygma, charism and sacrament needs to be actually embodied in the leadership of the local church if it is to come to life within the congregation. The key New Testament term for leadership in the local church is oversight ('episcopacy' is derived from the Greek noun). It carries the sense of guarding, protecting, knowing and nurturing. In the context of the church's 'immune system' it is clear that discernment must be one of the key gifts. Strong and unifying leadership will enable people in all three dimensions—by teaching and example to give them confidence to share their faith, to encourage and

model the use of spiritual gifts so that diversity builds up unity and to foster an atmosphere of expectancy and the numinous in worship which has a sacramental focus. In my own congregation, many people have found a fresh encounter with the Holy Spirit through the sacramental actions of anointing with oil and/or laying on of hands for healing and wholeness, and for some this has led on to more overtly charismatic experience. There is a great richness in this model as each element complements and enlivens the other. The diagram below suggests that the leadership of the church has a key role in holding all three priorities together in creative tension.

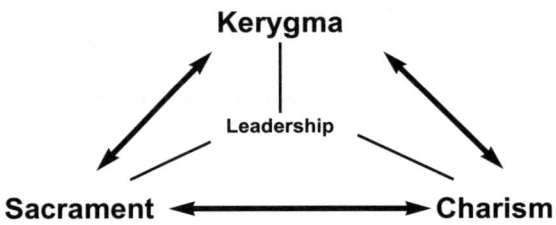

Worship is the point at which a congregation expresses its sense of identity, and perhaps the most significant step in enabling a convergence spirituality to enter the bloodstream of the local church is to practice 'convergence worship,' including all three areas of transformation in the regular experience of worship. As this process develops, so we should expect that the leadership, and in time the whole congregation, will grow in discernment. They are engaging in a spirituality of Word and Spirit which gives an alertness to the counterfeit, in the context of sacraments which are a continual reminder that any one local church is part of a much bigger whole and does not have an exclusive monopoly of the gospel.

For Anglicans, this 'bigger whole' is personified by the bishop, and I believe this model of convergence is also relevant to the episcopate. A deeply held instinct characteristic of the Church of England is inclusiveness. While there may be some historical factors at work here to do with the legal establishment of the church, this is clearly also a value of the gospel itself. But if it is to retain its integrity, an inclusive church needs especially vigilant leadership. Where there are no clear boundaries about who is in membership, there needs to be a spiritually strong centre so that the 'chief pastor'[17] can maintain direction and identity. The danger for the inclusive church comes when secular ideas of representation insinuate themselves with the demand that the spirituality of the leadership represents all the varied views of the membership, or even those who have very

---

17 The Ordinal, *ASB*, para 13, p 388.

little real connection with the church.

There are occasions when a bishop can use his institutional role to be a catalyst for unity and convergence. This was the case in a Team Ministry where following the mismanagement of an appointment, a great deal of negative energy was generated which threatened to be highly destructive. It was impossible to deal with at local level because certain people saw some of the clergy as part of the problem. Through the appointment of a competent and respected Team of Enquiry by the Bishop, recommendations were accepted which gave the clergy the security and support they needed to continue. At the same time the appointment of a Consultant to the Team began to enable people to work through areas of conflict and the scope for manipulation from the shadows was greatly reduced.

Churches which instinctively reject episcopal ministry may be denying themselves a vital element in their growth towards maturity, but the value of episcopacy has often been obscured because the power structures of the church have been subverted by the world. The authority of oversight in the church does not come from talent but by grace and service. Bonhoeffer draws out the essence of the New Testament's teaching when he writes 'One finds nothing whatsoever with regard to worldly charm and the brilliant attributes of a spiritual personality. The Bishop is a simple faithful man, sound in faith and life, who rightly discharges his duty to the church. His authority lies in the exercise of his ministry.'[18]

---

18 *Life Together*, p 85.

6
'On Earth as in Heaven'

In baptism every Christian is called to lifelong allegiance to Jesus Christ, to take part in the battle in which God himself is engaged—to liberate humankind from captivity to sin and death. The decisive victory has already been secured through the cross, but the war goes on. It is through the church that God has decreed that he will reveal his wisdom and dwell among his people. But the very vehicle God has chosen to bring freedom can itself be taken captive by the 'elemental spirits' (Gal.4.3), which manifest themselves in many different forms. I have attempted to draw out some of these manifestations without dwelling on the spiritual powers of darkness which lie behind them, but I believe we are going to see God releasing his Spirit in a new way, taking the church through the refining fires of conflict and awakening in his people a holy impatience for much more of his presence.

At his baptism, Jesus 'saw heaven being torn open and the Spirit descending upon him like a dove' (Mark 1.10). At this defining moment, both the passion and the gentleness of God are revealed. May God give us a passion to see that which veils his glory in the church being torn away and that essential gentleness that comes from a radical dependence upon his Holy Spirit.

> Set our feet on lofty places,
> Gird our lives that they may be
> Armoured with all Christlike graces
> In the fight to set men free.
> Grant us wisdom, grant us courage,
> That we fail not man nor thee.[19]

---

[19] From 'God of grace and God of glory,' H E Fosdick (1878-1969) *Hymns Ancient and Modern* (NS) No 367.